NO DOGS ON THE BED

First published in the UK in 2021 by Quiller, an imprint of Amberley Publishing.

British Library Cataloguing-in-Publication Data
A catalogue record for this book is available from the British Library.

ISBN 978-1-84689-350-6

Design by Guy Callaby

Printed in the Czech Republic

Quiller
An imprint of Amberley Publishing Ltd

The Hill, Merrywalks,
Stroud GL5 4EP
Tel: 01453 847800
Email: info@quillerbooks.com
Website: www.quillerpublishing.com

NO DOGS ON THE BED

John Holder

Quiller

For my wife Gaye, who loves cats

MOLLY OR HARRY, Lucy or Bertie, we adore our pooches and treat them as much-loved family members. We anthropomorphise them, and dress them in jackets, bandanas and bows. We pamper them and take them to grooming parlours. We kiss and cuddle them, mollycoddle and baby-talk to them, and buy them gifts that appeal to us. We tell them where we're going and when we'll be back, and we convince ourselves they understand. Well, they do, don't they?

But, as much as we love our dogs, they are, after all, dogs. They bark and whine, scratch and bite, chew, shed hair, steal and destroy. They lift their legs and squat at the most inappropriate of times, roll in dead things, and know just how to embarrass us with a quick hump, a sniff or a slobber ... or by dropping the deadliest of silent farts!

We accept their foibles, forgive their misdemeanours. tell them they're good and share the sofa with them. And that's because five hundred million of us around the world know the loyalty and reciprocated love of 'man's best friend'.

RADIO FLYER

"I don't think twice about picking up my dog's poop but if another dog's poop is next to it, I think 'Eww, dog poop!'."

Jonah Goldberg

"As a dog returns to his own vomit
so a fool repeats his folly."

Proverbs 26 verse 1

"You can trust a dog
to guard your home
but never trust a dog
to guard your dinner."

Anon

Sir Isaac Newton (1643 - 1727) invented the cat flap.

It also keeps dogs out.

"Anybody who doesn't know what soap tastes like, never washed a dog."

Franklin P. Jones

"Happiness is a warm puppy."

Charles M. Schulz

"Take a lesson from your dog. Shit happens;
kick grass over it and move on."

Anon

"The unspeakable in pursuit of the uneatable."

Oscar Wilde

WOOF

"Properly trained a man can be dog's best friend".

Corey Ford

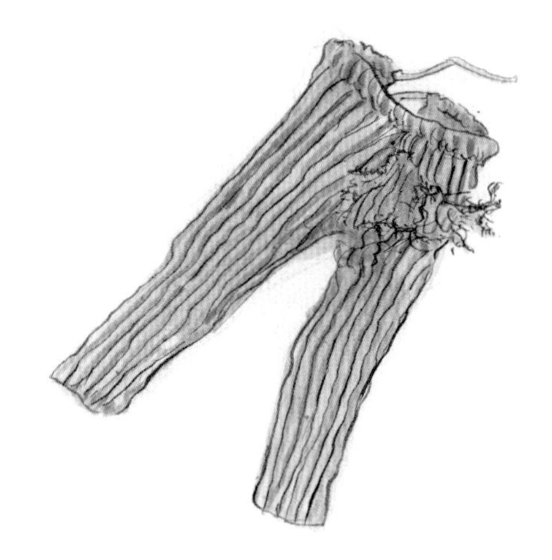

"Dachshunds are such beautiful
and sweet creatures and so full of tricks".

Queen Victoria

"A dog can't think that much about what it's doing, he just does what it feels like."

Barbara Kingsolver

ELECTRIC
FENCE

Loyalty

"I have seen a look in a dog's eyes, a quick vanishing look of amazed contempt and I am convinced that dogs think humans are nuts".

John Steinbeck

"Dogs got personality.
Personality goes a long way."

Quentin Tarantino

"What counts is not necessarily
the size of the dog in the fight,
it's the size of the fight in the dog."

Dwight D. Eisenhower

"It is nought good a slepying hound to wake."

Geoffrey Chaucer

Royal Mail

"Dogs are better than human beings because they know but don't tell."

Emily Dickinson

SPEYING
AND
NEUTERING
CLINIC

DOG TRAINING for BEGINNERS
VISA

Dog Obedience
This Certificate
is awarded to
Daisy
BEST IN SHOW

"Don't let the same dog bite you twice."

Chuck Berry

Get High on Bluegrass

"Every dog must have its day."

Jonathan Swift

"No dogs in the bed."

Andrew Johnston

10

"There has never been a happier, healthier and more loved dog than our Dilyn."

Carrie Symonds

"As fit as a butcher's dog."

John Camden Hotten, 1859

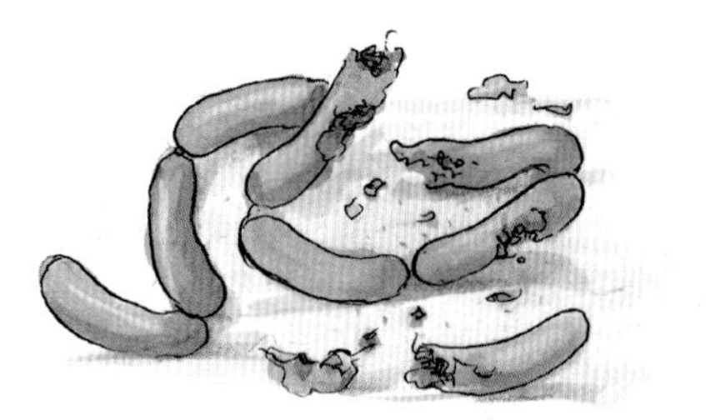

The Village Butcher

"You can't teach an old dog new tricks."

John Heywood, 1546

"Man is the only animal that blushes. Or needs to."

Mark Twain

"There is the little matter of disposal of droppings in which the cat is far ahead of it's rivals. The dog is somehow thrilled by what he or any of his friends have produced, hates to leave it, adores smelling it and sometimes eats it."

Paul Galico

*"Major is a sweet dog but is still adjusting to his surroundings."**

President Joe Biden

After Major bit a second member of White House staff.

"The greatest thing you'll ever learn
is just to love and be loved in return."

David Bowie

"Outside of a dog a book is man's best friend.
Inside of a dog is too dark to read."

Groucho Marx

"The better I get to know men

the more I find myself loving dogs."

Charles de Gaulle

POLICE DOG UNIT

"If aliens saw us walking our dogs
and picking up their poop,
who would they think is in charge."

Anon

SCOOP THE POOP

"The dog's kennel is not the place to keep a sausage."

Danish proverb